W9-CCO-922

BE MORE RBG

Written by Marilyn Easton

Contents

Introduction

**There are legends, there are icons,
and then there is RBG.**

Justice is best served with a little style, and
Ruth Bader Ginsburg does it better than anyone else.
From being one of only nine women who attended
Harvard Law School in 1956, through her 26 years
serving as the second female U.S. Supreme Court
Justice and everything in between, RBG has been
a pioneer in fighting sex-based discrimination and
standing up for what's right. And she's done it all
with peerless fairness, intelligence, and poise.

If you ever feel like progress (personal or political)
is a million miles away, look through these pages and
take inspiration from the Queen of the Supreme Court
herself. For guidance on speaking up in dissent,
balancing your time, or becoming the best—and/or
most notorious—version of yourself, this book will
answer the question: What would Ruth do? Whether
you're looking to change the world or find a
little change within yourself, you could
benefit from being more RBG.

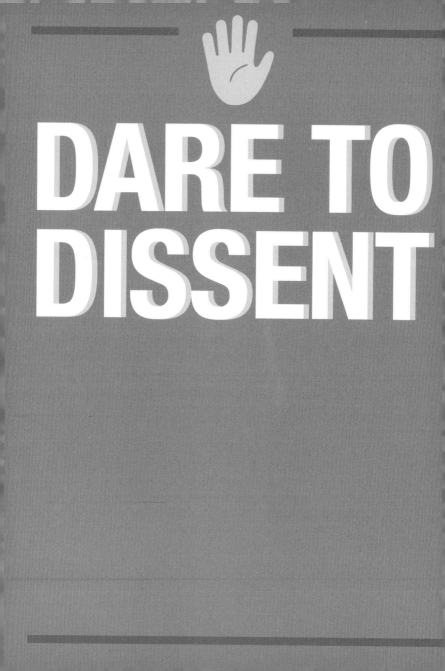

"SOME OF MY FAVORITE OPINIONS ARE DISSENTING OPINIONS."

"Dissents speak to a future age . . . the **greatest dissents** do become court opinions."

Speak up

Your voice is one of your most powerful tools, and no one has a right to silence it. Ruth has spent her whole career speaking up when it matters, and now her words on the Supreme Court are heeded across the world. Whether you're in a room with colleagues, classmates, or family, your thoughts matter. Don't be afraid to be heard, either to amplify the majority opinion, or as the lone dissenting voice.

RBG's first Supreme Court group photo.
— August '93

"I can say one thing about Justice Scalia: He is one of the few people in the world who can make me laugh, and I appreciate him for that."

Disagree
agreeably

RBG and Associate Justice Antonin Scalia
sat on the same bench for 23 years,
but rarely agreed on the cases put before
them. RBG listened to Scalia's more
conservative political opinions and used
them to strengthen her own arguments.
The pair even forged an unlikely
friendship off the bench. So don't brush
off individuals who think differently
to you. You might be surprised by the
common ground you can find when
you step outside your echo chamber.

disagree

"THIS IS MY DISSENTING COLLAR . . . IT LOOKS FITTING FOR DISSENTS."

Yellow majority
opinion collar

Favorite
everyday look

Surprise gift
from a fan

Collar with a pop
of color

Dissent with style

Inspired by Associate Justice Sandra Day O'Connor, RBG adds collars to her robes in place of the neckties worn by her male colleagues. However, RBG has taken accessorizing to the next level, collecting a wardrobe of sartorial signals that allow her to make her opinion known simply by her choice of collar. What you wear can be a symbol of your values, too. Whether you're sporting eco-friendly vintage pieces, ethically made fabrics, or wearing a t-shirt bearing a quote from RBG herself, you can also make a statement with your fashion.

"I'm sometimes asked when will there be enough women on the Supreme Court? And I say

WHEN THERE ARE NINE.

People are shocked.
But there'd been nine men, and nobody's ever raised a question about that."

Challenge the norm

RBG questions the status quo, whether it's through her written dissents or spoken opinions. Just because something has been done a certain way in the past, doesn't mean there isn't a better, different approach to take. And sometimes it takes a bold statement to make people realize that! For instance, RBG's vision of an all-female Supreme Court is likely shocking to some. But only by challenging the preconceptions of today can you hope to inspire lasting change for the future.

"When a thoughtless or unkind word is spoken, best tune out."

Block out the haters

RBG's job involves considering complex cases and crafting rigorous responses when necessary. This work requires Ruth's full and concentrated attention. She simply doesn't have time for unnecessary drama in her day, whether it's disagreements in the group chat or office gossip. Her attitude to negative energy is a reminder that anger, envy, and resentment are just a distraction from what's important. Whether you meditate, hit the gym, or play some opera through your noise-canceling headphones, find a way to rise above petty arguments. You'll soon feel more positive and more productive.

CHANGE
THE WORLD

"TIME IS ON THE SIDE OF CHANGE."

"Women belong in all places where decisions are being made ... It shouldn't be that women are the **exception**."

Open the door

When RBG attended Harvard Law School in 1956, there were just nine women in her class, compared to more than 500 men. With only one female bathroom available and a ban on women using certain spaces in the library, it was clear that female students were not welcome. But that didn't stop Ruth. RBG knows that to make a difference, you need to be in the room where change happens. Don't be afraid to forge a space for yourself; you'll be opening the doors for future leaders, too.

"Real change, enduring change, happens one step at a time."

Have patience

Ruth wasn't built in a day. After earning her law degree at Columbia in 1959, even RBG couldn't head directly to the Supreme Court. Over the following six decades, she has worked as a legal clerk, a research associate, a professor at two universities, general counsel for the American Civil Liberties Union, a fellow at Stanford University, and a judge. She has paid her dues and constantly deepened her understanding of the law. It is important to acknowledge that progress—personal and political— doesn't happen overnight. It takes both hard work and time but, don't fear—it will come.

"That's what I think a meaningful life is. One lives not just for oneself, but for one's community."

Think beyond yourself

Ruth may be one incredible individual, but her work impacts millions of people. When she gives her opinion, she is also speaking for those who don't have the power to. She knows that even her smallest actions can shape the lives of generations to come.

You might not be making constitution-defining decisions in your everyday life, but all of our actions have the potential to affect others. Be more like RBG and ask yourself every day what you can do to make this world a little better than it was the day before.

"President Obama? Well, let's say—*sympathique.* That's a French word. It means more than sympathetic. It means one who cares about other people."

Raise others up

RBG is happy to share the spotlight with others, especially those who support the same bright future that she does. Let's face it—although a sitting Supreme Court Justice is expected to remain publicly neutral about political personalities, sometimes you can't help calling it as you see it. When asked to describe President Barack Obama in one word, RBG wasn't afraid to share a positive judgement. Even those at the top of their game can benefit from a kind word or compliment, so don't hesitate to champion those around you.

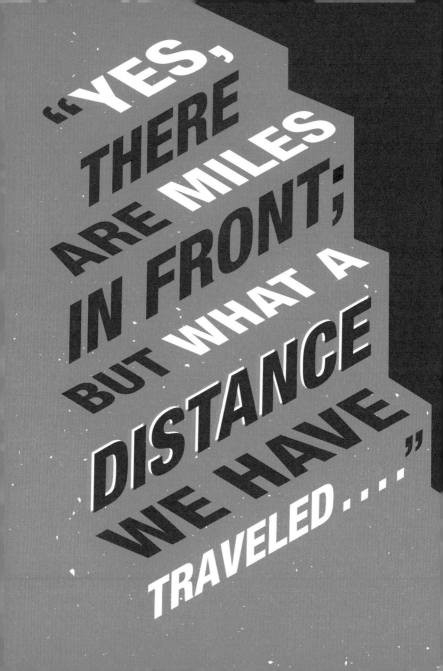

Celebrate success

When Ruth graduated law school at the top of her class, she was unable to secure an entry-level job at a law firm because of her gender. Now, she sits on the Supreme Court with two other female justices—the most that have ever occupied the bench at one time. Of course, there is always more progress to be made. However, taking a moment to acknowledge your accomplishments can be a powerful source of encouragement when it's time to take your next big step forward.

NOTORIOUS

"HOW DID I DECIDE TO BECOME A FLAMING FEMINIST LITIGATOR?"

"If confirmed, I will take that counsel to heart and strive to write opinions that both 'get it right' and 'keep it tight.'"

State your goals

Don't be afraid to set goals and state them out loud. Since RBG's confirmation to the Supreme Court in 1993, she's never shied away from following through on the promises she made at the start of her tenure. Whether you share your secret dream job ambitions with a friend, or post your New Year's resolutions online for all to see, it can be a powerful motivating tool to allow others to hold you to account. But, more importantly, it will encourage you to meet your own ambitions.

"YOU CAN TELL THEM I'LL BE BACK DOING PUSH-UPS NEXT WEEK."

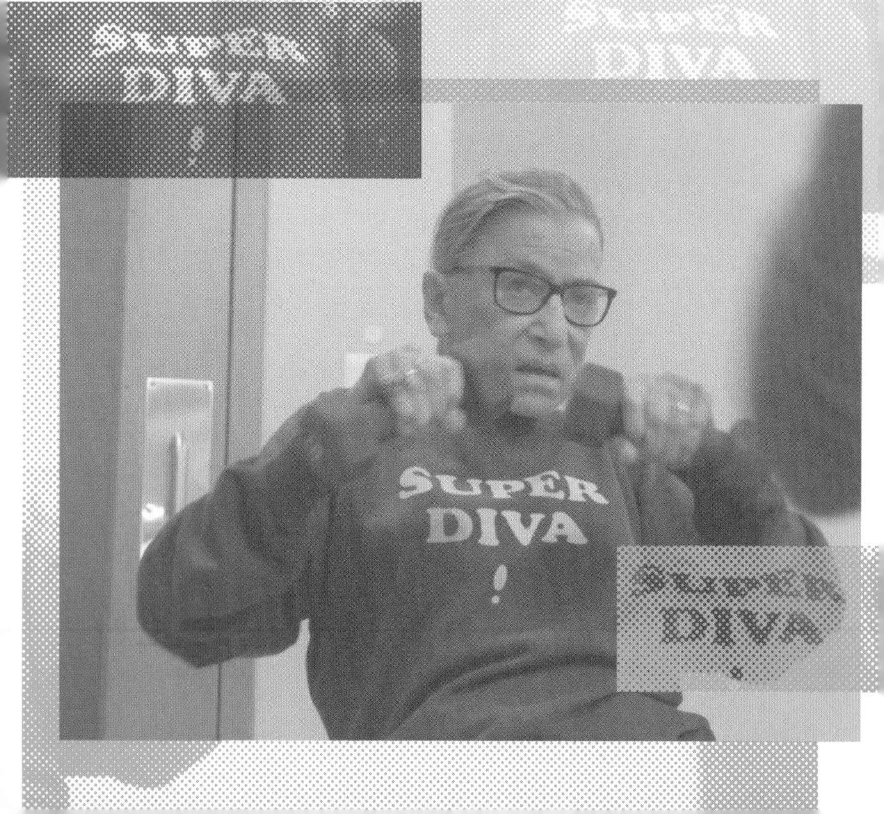

Work it out

As a three-time cancer survivor, Ruth stays strong
on and off the bench by hitting the gym. Nothing
stops RBG from making time for arm exercises with
her personal trainer—not even a heart stent. Ruth
knows self-care is all about taking small steps, so
start with a short set of push-ups and take a break
before heading into the next one. All it takes is
attitude, determination, and a motivational sweatshirt
to help you bench-press that extra pound.

#RBG #BeMoreRBG #SupremeQueen #Dissent

"I try to keep abreast of the latest that's on the Tumblr."

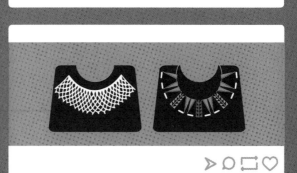

Stay on trend

You don't have to be an octogenarian to feel that the latest internet memes and social media stars are passing you by. It is easy to assume that, as an Associate Justice on the Supreme Court (and a grandmother), RBG might have dismissed her recent online fame as something trivial. But instead, she has embraced it. A new generation is celebrating RBG for the same qualities she has always embodied—but now with the addition of memes, merch, and a few hashtags. No one should be made to feel threatened by change; instead, see emerging trends as something exciting you can become a part of.

"IT'S GOT **ME** ON THE OTHER SIDE."

Don't be shy

Humility is important, but it's okay to love yourself
and take pride in your accomplishments. Whether
you've ruled in a case on gender equality or just
managed to get out of bed this morning, you deserve
to toot your own horn. RBG is proud to wear merch
such as t-shirts showcasing her own words of
wisdom—and her likeness. Don't shy away from
self-love. Who knows, maybe one day you'll get to
carry a tote bag with your face on it, too.

"Someone who used whatever **talent** she had to do her work to the **very best** of her ability."

Ruth's answer to the question:
"What would you like to be remembered for?"

Be legendary

RBG is undeniably iconic. She is the epitome
of class, feminism, and intellect, and she is
unapologetically herself. Her fans don't idolize
her for answering to them; they idolize her
because she answers only to herself (and the law).
She says what she means, she means what she
says, and she isn't afraid of a negative reaction.
Ruth did not show up to the Supreme Court
to sit back—she came to change the world.

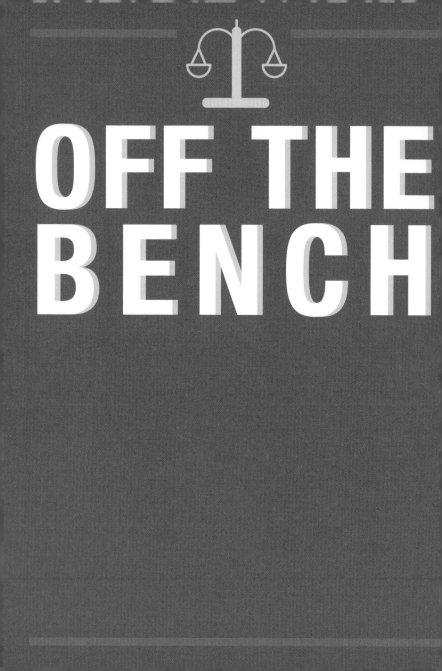

OFF THE BENCH

"IT'S HARD TO DO ANYTHING ALONE. "

"I had a life partner who thought my work was as important as his, and I think that made all the difference for me."

Find your Marty

Ruth and Marty were married for more than half a century and they are the ultimate when it comes to relationship goals. Marty was also a successful lawyer, but he believed supporting his wife in her work had been his life's greatest achievement. He saw that Ruth was the superhero the nation needed to fight inequality, so was happy to help her flourish. Accept the love you deserve and surround yourself with people who believe in you as much as you believe in them. Together, you'll be unstoppable.

"My success in law school . . . was in large measure because of baby Jane. I attended classes and studied diligently until 4 in the afternoon; the next hours were Jane's time . . .

After Jane's bedtime, I returned to the law books with renewed will. Each part of my life provided respite from the other . . . . "

Achieve the right balance for you

Like all of us, RBG is many things. She is a woman, a mother, a grandmother, a daughter, a wife, a Supreme Court Justice, a student of the law, and an icon. When Ruth started at law school, she was also the mother of a toddler. Ruth acknowledged that her life was more than just her studies and sought to use this to her advantage, finding a work-life balance that suited her along the way. Remember that many aspects of our lives connect to form one complete identity. Accept and embrace each part of yourself to keep your internal scales from tipping over.

"Most of the time . . . I'm thinking about legal problems. But when I go to the opera, I'm just lost in it . . . And I don't think about any legal brief."

Allow time for leisure

How can a cameo in an opera help you boss it in your day job? It seems counterintuitive, but taking time away from your everyday role to do something different can help you excel. RBG loves her position on the bench, spending countless hours immersed in court cases. But she also has a penchant for opera—watching it and even perfoming onstage. Getting lost in the music gives Ruth time to unwind and clear her head. Find a passion that makes you want to sing to the rafters. When you go back to the grind, you might even find a solution for the problem you were racking your brain over the day before.

#1 Bubbie

"Women will have achieved true equality when men share with them the responsibility of bringing up the next generation."

Share the load

You could do it all, but you don't have to! Ruth and Marty had two children together. They shared household responsibilities and took turns acting as the primary caregiver to allow the other to focus on their career. Once, after yet another phone call from his school regarding her son James's lively behavior, RBG reminded the school that James had two parents. Divvying up responsibilities—however small—allows both partners in a relationship time to focus on other goals.

"MY MOTHER TOLD ME TWO THINGS **CONSTANTLY.** ONE WAS TO **BE A LADY,** AND THE OTHER WAS TO BE INDEPENDENT. **"**

Seek guidance from others

Ruth has always been grateful to the leaders of the past, such as women's rights activist Susan B. Anthony and abolitionist and political activist Harriet Tubman. However, the woman she credits most for her accomplishments is her mother, Celia Bader. It's easy to be swayed by flash-in-the-pan influencers on social media, but try to find role models closer to home. The mentors you find within your communities will be those who inspire you in every aspect of your life for years to come.

SUPREME
WISDOM

"AS WE LIVE, WE CAN LEARN. IT'S IMPORTANT TO LISTEN."

"You can't have it all, all at once."

Take a breath

How can you take care of the world if you don't take care of yourself first? Ruth has a stellar work ethic and a reputation for not taking time off, but everyone deserves a break. Know when to take a breather from your work, studies, or fitness regime. After all, you can't be at the top of your game when you're tired and stressed. Take a moment to relax when you need to, even if that means a little snooze during the State of the Union address. With a little rest, you'll be able to accomplish everything you want to—just not all simultaneously!

"I'VE GOTTEN MUCH MORE **SATISFACTION** FOR THE THINGS THAT I'VE DONE FOR WHICH I WAS NOT PAID."

Pay it forward

Fame and fortune aren't everything—sometimes giving back is even more rewarding. RBG serves her country on the bench, but she still makes time to help her community in other ways. Ruth has volunteered her legal services countless times to protect the rights of those facing discrimination, and she inspires the next generation by speaking and reading to children. Not everything we do has monetary value, but the impact we have can be priceless.

"Fight for the things that you care about, but do it in a way that will lead others to join you."

Lead with integrity

It's okay to get fired up, especially when you're passionate about something. But if you want to get someone to fight for your cause, kicking, screaming, and bullying people isn't the way to do it. RBG knows it is essential to encourage the next generation of leaders to keep progress moving in the right direction. Those following her today are the leaders of tomorrow. Inspire people to get on your side with kindness, confidence, and meme-worthy wisdom.

I'm dejected, but only momentarily ...

You go on to the next challenge and you give it your all ...

There'll be another time, another day.

Never give up

Even if you hold one of the most senior positions
in the country, things won't always go your way.
Ruth is no stranger to being on the losing side of a
judicial decision. No matter how well-spoken you are
or how many facts you have in support of your cause,
you can't expect to win every argument. But that
doesn't mean you shouldn't put your best effort
into everything you do. Today you might hear "no,"
but the "yes" you've been waiting for could be
just around the corner.

"THERE IS STILL WORK TO BE DONE."

Keep on striving

Over her lifetime, Ruth has accomplished much to advance women's legal rights and protect against sex-based discrimination for all. RBG's incredible work ethic has kept her passionate every step of the way, but also accepting of the fact that there will always be more progress to be made. If we all strive to find that RBG spark and drive within ourselves, imagine what we could achieve.

Senior Editor Tori Kosara
Editor Beth Davies
Designer Stefan Georgiou
Editorial Assistant Nicole Reynolds
Pre-Production Producer Kavita Varma
Senior Producer Mary Slater
Managing Editor Sarah Harland
Design Manager Guy Harvey
Publisher Julie Ferris
Art Director Lisa Lanzarini
Publishing Director Simon Beecroft

Illustrations Stefan Georgiou, Guy Harvey, and Mark Penfound

DK would like to thank Megan Douglass and Julia March for
editorial assistance; Mark Penfound for additional design assistance;
and Taiyaba Khatoon for picture research.

First American Edition, 2019
Published in the United States by DK
Publishing 1450 Broadway, Suite 801,
New York, New York 10018

A WORLD OF IDEAS:
SEE ALL THERE IS TO KNOW
www.dk.com

Copyright © 2019 Dorling Kindersley Limited
DK, a Division of Penguin Random House LLC
19 20 21 22 23 10 9 8 7 6 5 4 3 2 1
001-317006-Oct/2019

All rights reserved. Without limiting the rights
under the copyright reserved above, no part
of this publication may be reproduced, stored
in, or introduced into a retrieval system,
or transmitted, in any form, or by any means
(electronic, mechanical, photocopying, recording,
or otherwise), without the prior written permission
of the copyright owner. Published in Great Britain
by Dorling Kindersley Limited.

A catalog record for this book is available
from the Library of Congress.

ISBN: 978-1-4654-9218-0

Printed and bound in China

The publisher would like to thank the following for
their kind permission to reproduce their photographs:

(Key: a-above; b-below/bottom; c-center; f-far;
l-left; r-right; t-top) 6-7 Getty Images: Diana
Walker / The LIFE Images Collection. 6 Getty
Images: Diana Walker / The LIFE Images Collection.
20 Getty Images: Bettmann. 24 Getty Images: Pool /
Getty Images News (b). 32 Rex by Shutterstock:
Kobal / Cnn Films (t, b, cl, crb). 36 Rex by
Shutterstock: AP. 48 Rex by Shutterstock: AP (t). 54
Getty Images: Alex Wong / Getty Images News (t).
56 Alamy Stock Photo: ZUMA Press Inc (b). 62 Getty
Images: Allison Shelley / Stringer /
Getty Images News

Cover image: Back: Getty Images:
Chip Somodevilla/Staff

All other images © Dorling Kindersley

For further information see: www.dkimages.com